W9-CBU-243

I HAVE OCD.
NOW WHAT?

CARLA MOONEY

ROSEN
PUBLISHING®

New York

Published in 2016 by The Rosen Publishing Group, Inc.
29 East 21st Street, New York, NY 10010

Library of Congress Cataloging-in-Publication Data

Mooney, Carla, 1970-
I have OCD. Now what?/Carla Mooney.
     pages cm.—(Teen life 411)
Includes bibliographical references and index.
Audience: Grades 7–12
ISBN 978-1-4994-6140-4 (library bound)
1. Obsessive-compulsive disorder—Popular works. I. Title.
RC533.M62 2016
616.85'227—dc23

                                              2014041867

Manufactured in the United States of America

CONTENTS

When he was about eight years old, Benjamin Shapiro developed a fear of being kidnapped. While many kids share the same fear, Benjamin's grew until he was consumed with an unfounded phobia of being abandoned by his parents or being left an orphan. To relieve his anxiety, Benjamin created several rituals. He would touch objects a certain number of times and in a particular way. By doing so, he believed that he could keep his world safe and his parents unharmed. Benjamin says that he hated the rituals but felt as if he needed them. According to him, performing the rituals made him feel protected. Benjamin shared his story in a May 2014 article for *Psychology Today*. He explained his former thought patterns, saying, "If I touch my doorknob now eight times, Mom and Dad will come home unharmed. If I read the same page six times in a row, I won't be orphaned." Concerned, Benjamin's parents took him to see a therapist. The therapist diagnosed him with a mental disorder called obsessive-compulsive disorder (OCD).

By the time Benjamin was twelve years old, OCD was controlling his life. He had to leave

With obsessive-compulsive disorder, irrational thoughts or impulses repeatedly invade a person's mind, no matter how much he or she tries to stop them.

school for four months and work with tutors and therapists as he tried to deal with his uncontrollable thoughts. When one of his therapists asked Benjamin to list his obsessions, the list covered several pages. He shares that he felt compelled to touch objects repeatedly until he felt "just right." His rituals calmed his anxiety. However, thinking about his obsessions and performing the rituals took up a great deal of time and significantly impaired his life.

Fear and anxiety are parts of everyone's life. However, for some people, fear and anxiety can turn into something more serious—obsessive-compulsive disorder. According to the National Institute of Mental Health (NIMH), approximately 2 percent of the U.S. population will be diagnosed with OCD at some point in their lives. That's nearly one out of every forty Americans. OCD is generally diagnosed when a person experiences obsessions and compulsions that interfere with daily life for more than one hour a day. Obsessions are irrational thoughts or impulses that repeatedly appear in a person's mind. Because they are unwanted, these obsessions generally cause a person to feel anxiety. These obsessions persist, despite a person's efforts to get rid of them by ignoring, controlling, or suppressing them. To reduce the anxiety caused by obsessions, a person might repeat a ritual or repetitive action such as washing his or her hands or counting objects. These compulsive actions are meaningless to others. Over time, the obsessions and compulsions of OCD greatly interfere with a person's ability to lead a normal life.

Although OCD is a serious mental disorder, it can be treated. The most common OCD treatment is generally some form of psychotherapy, also known as talk therapy. In some cases, medication may also be used to treat OCD. With treatment plans, most people with OCD are able to live productive lives.

Today, Benjamin is a seventeen-year-old living in New York City. He says that treatment has allowed him to manage his OCD and live like a typical teenager. He has returned to school and participates in sports and other extracurricular activities. Benjamin hopes to inspire others, saying, "I know what it feels like to be trapped in your own head . . . While there may be no cure, there is hope. True, the only way around is through. But someone like me made it to the other side."

WHAT IS OBSESSIVE-COMPULSIVE DISORDER?

Everyone feels the urge to double-check things occasionally. You might double-check to make sure you put your keys in your pocket or purse. Or you might double-check to make sure you turned off the oven or locked the door before leaving the house. For the majority of people, these feelings of small doubts or uncertainty are perfectly normal and healthy. For others, however, these feelings can become overwhelming and grow into something much more serious.

Obsessive-compulsive disorder (OCD) is a disorder that affects the brain and behavior. People suffering from OCD might have certain thoughts over and over again. Called obsessions, these frequently upsetting thoughts cause severe anxiety and distress. Attempting to control the obsessions, many people with OCD feel an overwhelming urge, or compulsion, to perform certain rituals or routines. Eventually, these thoughts and behaviors begin to control them, taking over their lives and interfering with daily activities. They may perform these routines repeatedly, often consuming a large part of their daily schedules.

A woman with OCD cannot escape the fear that she has lost her keys. She will repeatedly check her purse to make sure the keys are safe.

Hand washing is a common ritual performed by some people with OCD. Their obsession with germs and cleanliness drives them to wash their hands constantly.

Having OCD is like having your mind stuck on a particular thought or image. For example, for a young man with OCD, thoughts about germs or dirt might cause him to experience feelings of severe anxiety. To reduce this anxiety, he might then develop a ritual of washing his hands repeatedly. Performing the ritual produces a temporary relief from the anxiety caused by the thoughts of germs and dirt. Still, performing the ritual is not pleasurable. The young man is stuck in this routine and cannot stop, even if his skin becomes raw and bleeds from overwashing. For this reason, OCD is sometimes known as the doubting disease. While everyone experiences doubt and uncertainty at times, for people with OCD, these feelings cause severe and uncontrollable anxiety.

Twenty-two-year-old Josh Cannings suffers from a type of OCD called symmetry OCD. People with symmetry OCD often feel the need to perform tasks in a symmetrical, orderly, or balanced way. For example, they may need to align objects in a particular way or, as in the case of Cannings, repeat the same action with both hands, both feet, or both sides of the body. The subject of a BBC television documentary in 2013, Cannings explained that everywhere he goes he must

touch everything with both his right and left hands and feet an equal number of times. If he picks up a fork with his left hand, he must touch it with his right hand, too. If he does not touch something equally with both sides of his body, he is overcome by a feeling of dread. The dread has a physical effect, too, causing anxiety, sweating, an increased heart rate, and heavy breathing. To keep the dread at bay, he continually performs his rituals. On one trip to a movie theater, Cannings said that he accidentally brushed his left hand on the wall. He left the theater because he did not want to draw attention to his disorder. However, an hour later his compulsion forced him to return to the theater so that he could touch the same wall with his right hand.

OBSESSIONS AND COMPULSIONS

People who have OCD experience obsessions and compulsions. Obsessions are persistent, intrusive, and unwanted thoughts, images, or urges. The obsessions are replayed in their minds over and over, no matter what they do. Those who suffer from OCD do not want to keep having these thoughts, but they cannot stop or control them. While someone with OCD usually knows that his or her obsession doesn't make sense and that it is not reasonable, his or her feelings are nevertheless very real and intense.

While obsessions occur in the mind, compulsions are those physical behaviors that a person repeatedly performs in order to reduce the anxiety caused by his or her obsessions. Compulsions vary from person to person. Some common compulsions include counting, washing, touching, and checking, which will be discussed in more detail in a later section. The severity and duration of obsessions and compulsions are different for each person.

Jeff Bell, a San Francisco radio broadcaster and author of two books about his experiences with OCD, says that the disorder filled him with fears of unintentionally harming others. As a result, he was unable to drive a car because every time the car hit a bump, he was devastatingly afraid that he had run

In some cases, OCD can be severe enough to disrupt a person's daily life, including his or her ability to run errands, maintain a social life, or even drive a car.

over somebody. Every time, he would feel compelled to stop the car, get out, and check that he had not, in fact, hurt anybody. Sometimes, Bell's OCD even interfered with his ability to walk to work. If he came across a twig on the sidewalk, he would be concerned that if he did not move the twig, someone might be harmed by it. However, at the same time, he would worry that moving the twig could cause someone else to be injured who would have been fine had he left the twig where it initially was. These types of uncontrollable irrational thoughts flooded Bell's mind. While this thinking sounds ridiculous to somebody who is not afflicted with OCD, it is characteristic of those living with the disorder.

In many situations, performing a ritual is perfectly normal. For example, many sports players have rituals they perform before or during a game to bring good luck. Minor routines that do not interfere with people's abilities to carry on with their lives are perfectly normal. However, for a person diagnosed with OCD, these routines can be compulsive behaviors in response to overpowering obsessions—ones that cause significant distress and interfere with his or her ability to live a normal life.

Signs and Symptoms

Everyone has occasional doubts or the urge to double-check something. We all perform small rituals to reduce anxiety. Feeling doubts or anxiety from time to time

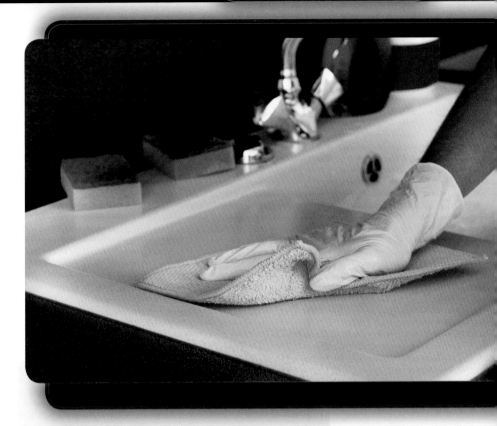

While cleaning can be a normal routine for many people, for those with OCD, cleaning routines can become excessive and interfere with daily life.

and carrying out minor routines to cope with them is completely normal. It is when these thoughts and behaviors cause intense distress and interfere with daily life that they may be signs of OCD. No two people experience OCD the same way. Some have a fear of germs or dirt. Others cannot stop thinking about acts of violence, such as hurting loved ones. Some people with OCD think constantly about certain sexual acts. Others have urges to

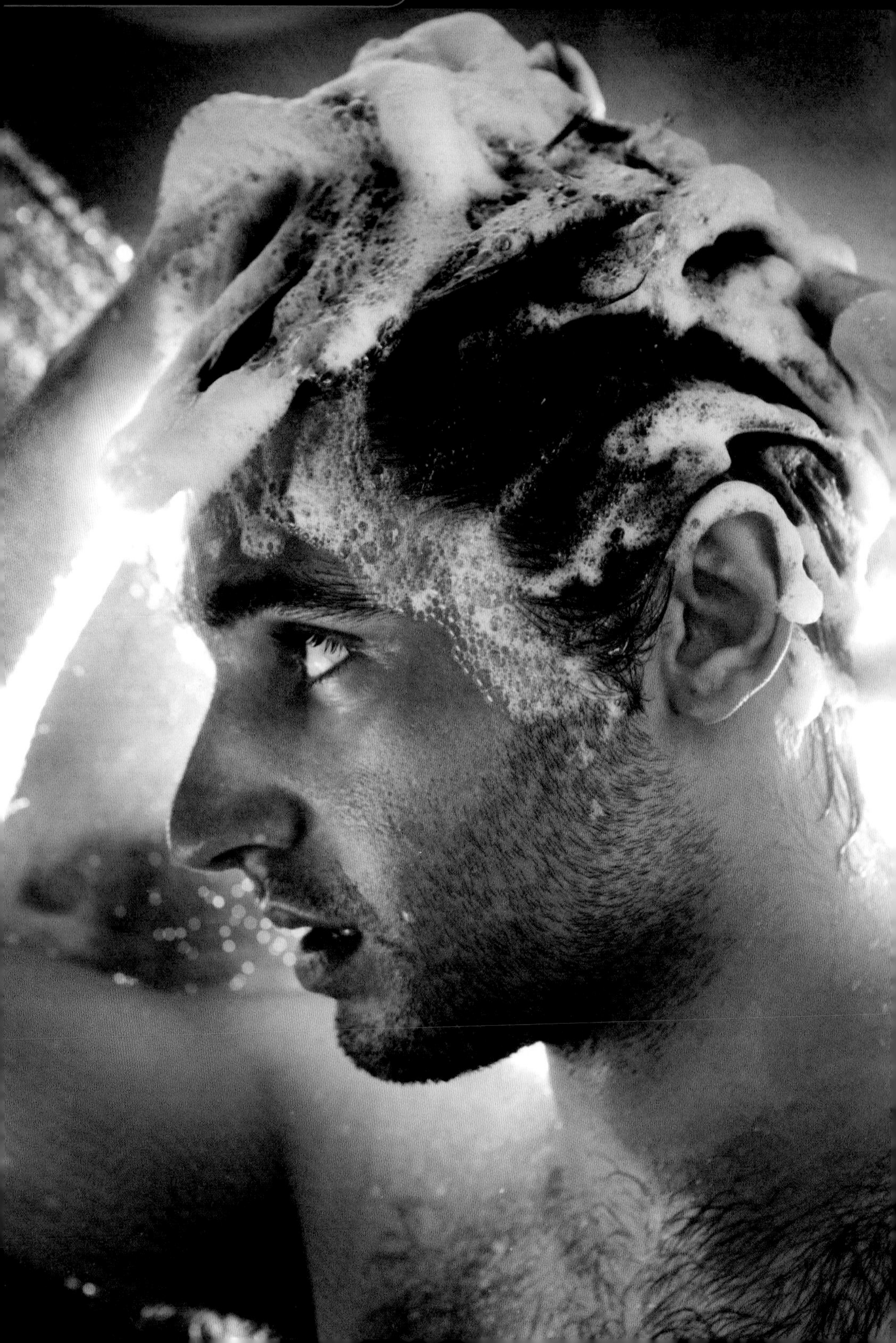

keep everything around them neat and ordered. In order to deal with these obsessive thoughts, people with OCD perform the same practices repeatedly. They may wash their hands multiple times, lock and unlock the same doors, count things around them, hold on to unnecessary items, or retrace the same steps over and over again.

Over the course of a person's lifetime, symptoms of OCD may come and go. He or she may be better at times and worse at others. In general, however, people with OCD spend at least one hour a day consumed with their thoughts and rituals. Many spend much more time—up to several hours each day—focusing on obsessive thoughts and the compulsive rituals that arise from them. Their obsessions and compulsions get in the way of daily life, interfering with their normal routines, schoolwork, jobs, family lives, and social activities.

Amy Iannuzzi-Tingley from Norfolk, Virginia, suffers from OCD that manifests as an obsession with germs. At its worst, she says that her obsession with germs compelled her to take three scalding hot showers a day and to wash her hands at least fifty times a day. Amy says that she first began showing signs of OCD around age eleven when she started washing and showering more frequently. At first, she did not realize what she was doing. When she saw a television show that featured people talking about their experiences with OCD, Amy

An obsession with germs can compel a person with OCD to take multiple showers each day and wash his or her hands more than fifty times each day.

realized that she might have the disorder. She did not tell her family or friends or seek medical help. Instead, Amy hid her OCD throughout middle and high school, making excuses when people noticed her washing her hands or changing her clothes. She says that her obsession with germs and compulsions to wash, clean,

Obsessive-Compulsive Personality Disorder

Sometimes mistaken for OCD, obsessive-compulsive personality disorder (OCPD) is a personality disorder that involves a preoccupation with orderliness, perfectionism, and control in almost every part of a person's life. People with OCPD may spend hours cleaning their homes so that they are perfect. They may become irritated if someone disturbs the orderliness. People with OCPD often display a rigid adherence to rules and regulations. They are unwilling to give responsibilities to others and feel that their way of doing things is the only "right way."

OCPD differs from OCD in several ways. While people with OCD realize that their thoughts and behaviors are irrational, people with OCPD believe that their actions and thoughts are completely normal and justified. In many cases, this rigidness may make them more efficient at performing certain tasks, but it often interferes with personal relationships. Unlike people with OCD who want their tortured thoughts to stop, people with OCPD generally do not believe they need treatment. They are convinced that everything would be all right if everyone around them simply followed their rules. People diagnosed with OCPD can learn to manage their symptoms with treatment, especially psychotherapy with a trained mental health professional.

and avoid touching potentially dirty objects took over her life. When Amy moved away for college, however, her OCD overwhelmed her. In class, she could not touch a test paper because she worried it was contaminated with germs. She was forced to withdraw from school after only five weeks. At that point, Amy was officially diagnosed with OCD and entered a treatment program. With treatment, Amy learned to manage her OCD.

If left untreated, OCD interferes with a person's daily life, affecting work, school, and relationships with others. Family and friends often feel frustrated, guilty, or angry when dealing with a person with OCD. Many wonder why the person cannot just get over his or her obsessions or stop performing certain behaviors. They may not understand that OCD is not a choice. It is an illness like heart disease, diabetes, or asthma and requires long-term treatment and support.

WHO IS AT RISK?

According to the National Institute of Mental Health (NIMH), about 2.2 million American adults have OCD. OCD affects men and women in approximately equal numbers. For many people, the signs and symptoms of OCD begin in childhood. In fact, according to the NIMH, about one-third of adults with OCD began to experience symptoms as a child. For others, symptoms develop later in adolescence or early adulthood. For some people, OCD symptoms emerge gradually.

Working together in a group therapy session, several participants talk about different strategies that they use to recognize and manage symptoms of OCD.

For others, a specific event can trigger onset. By age nineteen, most people with OCD have received an official diagnosis of the disorder.

OCD also tends to run in families. People with a close family member, such as a sibling, parent, or child, with the disorder are more likely to develop OCD themselves. In some cases, however, a person can develop OCD without any family history of the disorder.

TREATMENT IS AVAILABLE

Although OCD is a serious disorder, it can be treated. If you suspect that you or someone you know has OCD, you should seek help from a health care professional such as a doctor or mental health expert. These professionals can diagnose and determine the best treatment plan for people with OCD. Treatment of the disorder can involve psychotherapy, medication, or a combination of the two. Working closely with a health care professional to decide on the best treatment plan, most people can manage their OCD so that it does not control their lives and enjoy an improved quality of life.

Nearly twelve years after withdrawing from college, Amy is living a normal life and working as a speech pathologist. She still has OCD, but treatment has allowed her to manage the disorder. She makes sure that she is not washing her hands too much or excessively avoiding things that may be dirty. Instead, she washes her hands only before cooking and after using the bathroom and showers once a day. As an advocate for OCD awareness, Amy reaches out to others with the disorder. She started a support group and participates in talks and lectures about living with OCD. She says that she wants to show other people with OCD that there is treatment for the disorder and hope for a normal life.

MYTH

All people with OCD are neat and orderly.

FACT

OCD covers a wide range of obsessions and compulsive behaviors. Although some people with OCD wash constantly because they are concerned with dirt and germs, being neat is not necessarily a symptom of the disorder.

MYTH

OCD is a very rare disorder.

FACT

OCD is one of the most common mental disorders in the United States, affecting more than 2.2 million Americans, according to the National Institute of Mental Health.

MYTH

Children do not get OCD.

FACT

According to the International OCD Foundation, at least one in two hundred children and teenagers have OCD, which is about the same number of children and teenagers with diabetes.

MYTHS AND FACTS

CHAPTER 2

DIFFERENT TYPES OF OCD

Most people who have OCD suffer from both obsessions and compulsions. Obsessions and compulsions can take almost any form. As a result, there is no "typical" or "normal" OCD. Each individual's experience with the disorder is unique and personal. Some people have obsessions with contamination and cleanliness. Others may have uncontrollable urges to check on or organize personal items. Although OCD can manifest differently for different people, there are several common categories of symptoms that specialists have noted.

CONTAMINATION AND CLEANING

One of the most common obsessions for people with OCD is a fear of contamination. People who have this form of OCD may fear becoming sick, making others sick, or both. Some fear all illnesses, while others fear specific diseases, such as AIDS, cancer, or influenza. People who experience contamination obsessions are frequently disturbed by concerns that they accidentally touched things with germs or that they may transfer germs to someone or something else. Some of the most common symptoms associated with contamination obsessions include a fear of bodily wastes or fluids, dirt, germs, environmental contaminants, things that are sticky or greasy, or contact with animals. Other common symptoms include fear of illness, hospitals, or anyone who is or appears to be sick.

People with this type of OCD may feel a compulsive need to clean or wash themselves to avoid contamination

The fear of contamination can lead some people to worry about touching objects with potential germs. Often, they engage in rituals of cleaning and avoidance to manage their fear.

with germs. To ease their anxiety, they might engage in excessive hand washing, bathing, or disinfecting. In some cases, the person may wash so often that he or she damages his or her skin. Some use barriers such as gloves, paper, or plastic to avoid directly touching objects or people.

Science writer David Adam suffers from OCD and a fear of contracting HIV. In an April 2014 article he wrote for the *Guardian*, he describes how his obsessions and compulsions affect his life, "I obsess about ways that I could catch AIDS. I compulsively check to make sure I haven't caught HIV, and I steer my behaviour to make sure I don't catch it in future. I see HIV everywhere. It lurks on toothbrushes and towels, taps and telephones. I wipe cups and bottles, hate sharing drinks, and cover every scrape and graze with multiple plasters." Like most people struggling with OCD, he knows that his fears are unfounded. He says, "My rational self knows that these fears are ridiculous. I have a PhD in chemical engineering and for most of my career have been a science writer . . . I know that I can't catch AIDS in those situations. But still the thoughts and the anxiety come." Adam's case is typical for this type of OCD.

Harm-Related Obsessions and Checking Compulsions

Checking that you have done something is a normal part of life. You check to make sure you have your car keys. You check to make sure that you have locked the

A person with a checking compulsion may compulsively check to make sure the door is locked, fearing that an intruder will break in if he or she does not check multiple times.

door or turned off the stove. For most people, checking something once is enough to put their mind at ease. However, for people with checking compulsions, the need to check something repeatedly may compel them to check something dozens or even hundreds of times.

Often a checking compulsion is driven by a fear of harming oneself or others. People with checking compulsions fear that something bad might happen because they were careless or made mistakes. They worry about harming themselves or others or damaging property. For example, somebody with this type of OCD may worry that if he or she doesn't lock the door properly, an intruder will break into the house. Or someone might worry that if he or she forgets to turn off the stove, his or her house will burn down and everyone inside will be killed. People with this form of OCD feel a heavy anxiety that their actions could lead to tragedy.

In order to control these harm-related obsessions, many people with this form of OCD have a compulsion to check things. Through repeated checking, they try to control the world around them and quell their fears. They may excessively check faucets, stoves, the locks on doors and windows, or lights. Others repeatedly review their own words to make sure they haven't said anything hurtful or offensive.

Many people with harm-related obsessions worry that they will injure people while driving. Some drive the same routes over and over to make sure that they did not previously hit people by accident and then leave them injured in the road. Driving over a minor

Having repetitive behaviors does not always mean that a person has OCD. Impulse control disorders also involve repetitive behaviors. Typical impulse control behaviors include compulsive gambling, compulsive shopping, compulsive stealing, and drug addictions. People with impulse control disorders often have a hard time stopping harmful, obsessive activities. One important difference between OCD and impulse control disorders is how the behavior makes the person feel. For people with OCD, the compulsive thought or behavior makes them upset or distraught; they do not enjoy their behavior. In contrast, people with impulse control disorders generally enjoy their compulsive behavior while they are engaged in it (although many do feel guilty afterward).

IMPULSE CONTROL DISORDERS VS. OCD

bump in the road can trigger a fear of having struck a person. Even if they get out of the car to check the road to make sure there is no injured person, they may watch the news for days, looking for any hit-and-run accidents in their area.

Other people with harming obsessions have difficulty writing. They obsess over misspelling or omitting words or making other mistakes. They become anxious if they do not check what they have written repeatedly. They fall into an endless loop of writing, checking, and rewriting.

Anne Coulter's OCD symptoms emerged in her early twenties. She began performing checking rituals to make

sure everything was safe. In an interview with Health. com, Coulter described her symptoms: "When it first started, I'd check the locks and stove a few times. As time went by, I started checking more and more things— the iron, the hair dryer, the window-screen locks—and I'd check them each dozens of times before leaving for work and before going to bed. At its worst, the checking and re-checking took three to four hours a day."

Coulter also described the doubts that flooded her mind. Even after checking that something such as the stove was turned off, Coulter would then grow concerned that she may have bumped into the knob and turned it back on. She would check again.

SEXUAL AND AGGRESSIVE OBSESSIONS

Another category of OCD obsessions includes those that are aggressive or sexual in nature. People with aggressive obsessions may have uncontrollable thoughts of hurting themselves. Others become obsessed with the thought of harming another person even though they do not actively desire to. They might have constant thoughts of dead or injured bodies entering their minds. Others may have more specific fears, such as a fear of pushing someone in front of an oncoming train or car. One

The compulsion to check constantly that the stove and other appliances are turned off is driven by the fear that something bad will happen if the person does not check several times.

patient with OCD reported that she could not stop constant thoughts and images of choking young children to death from appearing in her head. It is important to clarify that she did not actively want to harm children. In fact, because she was afraid that she would act on these thoughts, she avoided all children entirely.

People with sexual obsessions may experience unwanted thoughts of sexual activity with family members, friends, or strangers. They might obsess about sexually molesting another person against his or her will. They also might obsess over specific sexual acts. Again, it is important to note that a person with this type of OCD will not necessarily follow through on his or her sexual thoughts. In fact, instead of enjoying these thoughts, people with sexual or aggressive obsessions often want to make these thoughts stop.

Sexual and aggressive obsessions can be extremely disturbing for those who suffer from them. Many people believe that simply having these thoughts makes them bad people. People who fear hurting themselves may go to great extremes to avoid certain objects or situations. They may cope by engaging in rituals and behaviors to protect themselves and others from harm.

PERFECTIONISM AND SYMMETRY OBSESSIONS AND COMPULSIONS

Some people with OCD find themselves with an obsessive need to have objects arranged in a precise order that makes sense to them. While it is healthy to want to

A person with a symmetry compulsion may feel the
need to make sure objects are lined up in a perfect
order or evenly spaced.

live and work in a clean, neat environment, people with
this form of OCD become obsessed with symmetry and
arranging things perfectly. Objects might be arranged
by size, color, subject, number, or some other crite-
ria. These individuals can spend hours organizing and
arranging everything from books to cans of soup. When
they are unable to arrange things to their satisfaction

or if somebody moves something out of order, they can become irritated and distressed.

Other people with a similar form of OCD are obsessed with keeping everything even or symmetrical. For example, a person with a compulsion to even things out may chew food an equal number of times on each side of his or her mouth. If the person bumps his right arm against a wall, he may feels as if he needs to walk through the room again and bump his left arm. Josh Cannings, whose personal story was addressed earlier, has this type of OCD.

Some people with OCD feel a strong need to do things perfectly. For example, they want objects placed in specific places and become distressed if they are not perfectly placed. They may spend hours adjusting objects until they are precisely aligned, even though friends and family cannot detect the difference. Students with OCD may spend hours on homework, doing it over and over until it is perfect.

Many people with this type of OCD are so consumed with arranging and perfectionism that they spend hours on it. For example, a person with OCD who is obsessed with putting down a bag in just the "right way" might spend hours putting the bag down over and over until it feels right.

RELIGIOUS OBSESSIONS

Another form of OCD is experienced by people with religious obsessions. This type of OCD can affect people

A person with a religious obsession prays repeatedly on his knees in order to reduce anxiety. This type of OCD, in which sufferers become convinced that they are not devout enough, can affect people from all religions.

of all faiths. They frequently worry about strict adherence to their religious traditions. Many become anxious with the thought that if they make a single mistake they will be condemned to punishment such as hell.

In addition to obsessing about following religious rituals perfectly, a person with a religious obsession may worry about having immoral or sinful thoughts. They worry about past actions that they consider sinful and fear that they will be punished yet by God for their thoughts and actions. In order to reduce anxiety, a person with religious obsessions may pray excessively or in a particular way. Some feel a compulsion to confess minor actions that they believe are sins to a priest, a rabbi, or some other religious authority.

HOARDING OBSESSIONS

Hoarding can be another symptom of OCD as well as several other mental disorders. People who hoard have a compulsion to collect and save large quantities of items. Because they are often unable to determine what objects are necessary or useful, they save everything. Those suffering from a compulsion to hoard often worry that if they throw things away, they will someday need those things. Rather than risk not having an item when he or she needs it, the person saves it.

People with OCD can hoard any type of item. Commonly hoarded items include newspapers, magazines, empty boxes, old greeting cards, string, rubber bands, and containers. Excessive hoarding usually causes problems with family members when they object to living in the growing chaos and clutter. If family members attempt to throw away items, the person who hoards may become frantic and distraught.

OTHER SYMPTOMS OF OCD

Not everyone's symptoms fall neatly into one of the main categories of OCD. Obsessive-compulsive disorder is an incredibly individual disease. It can vary greatly from person to person. Some people with OCD have compulsions to touch, tap, or rub objects. Others have compulsions to count or repeat numbers, words, or phrases. Some constantly ask for reassurance. Others engage in mental rituals that are not easily observed by outsiders.

OCD, in all its forms, is a chronic mental disorder that should be taken seriously. If you suspect that you or someone you know may have OCD, you should seek help from a mental health professional.

CHAPTER 3

WHAT CAUSES OCD?

There is no single, determined cause for why some people develop obsessive-compulsive disorder. OCD can strike people of any age, gender, race, or social background. Most experts believe that a combination of biology, genetics, and environmental factors interact to influence whether someone develops OCD.

While having a risk factor may increase a person's chances of developing OCD, it does not mean that a person will necessarily develop the disorder. Many people with risk factors for OCD never develop it. Nonetheless, knowing the risk factors can help a person recognize whether he or she is more likely to develop OCD. With this knowledge, the person can learn about the disorder, its symptoms, and treatments.

BIOLOGICAL FACTORS

Many scientists believe that OCD has a biological basis. Some researchers believe that differences in brain structure and how the brain works may be factors in the development of OCD. Everyone thinks strange thoughts or worries at times. However, most people dismiss these thoughts and move on with their day-to-day lives. For most people, these thoughts are like junk mail in the brain. Most people's brains have a filter that catches the junk mail and throws it away. For a person with OCD, however, the brain's spam filter has stopped working. Random thoughts are not filtered and keep coming. They can quickly outnumber the important messages in the brain. Eventually, a person with OCD can become overwhelmed.

Sophisticated brain imaging such as positron emission tomography (PET) and functional magnetic resonance imaging (fMRI) allows researchers to look closely at the working brain. Using these technologies, researchers can see the changes that take place in the brain during different tasks or situations. Researchers have found that several areas of the brain may be connected to the symptoms of OCD. Scans have found that people with OCD have abnormal activity in certain areas of the brain that are associated with anxiety, habit formation, and skill learning. These areas include the orbitofrontal cortex and the anterior cingulate cortex in the front of the brain and the striatum and thalamus in the deeper parts of the brain. These areas form a circuit. The repeated unpleasant thoughts and feelings of OCD may develop when there is a problem in communication between the areas of the brain on this circuit. "There are a lot of neuroimaging studies in OCD that suggest that the connections between regions of the brain are different in people who have OCD," says Dr. Dorothy Grice, a professor of psychiatry at Mount Sinai Hospital, in New York City, in a July 2013 interview with the *New York Daily News*. She continues, "Once we understand the underlying circuits that have gone awry, we

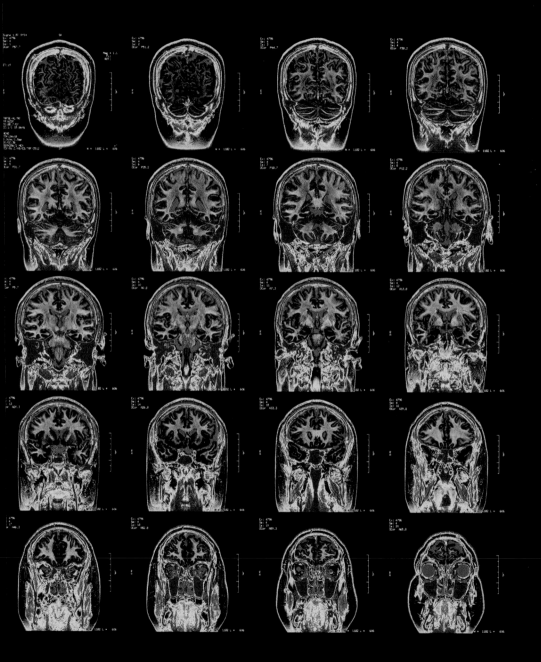

can think about what kind of interventions would be more specific to OCD."

Research has identified other parts of the brain that are different in people with OCD. Scans have shown that parts of the basal ganglia are smaller in people with OCD than people who do not have the disorder. The basal ganglia are associated with several brain functions, including control of voluntary motor movements and routine behaviors or habits. Scans of children with OCD reveal a larger thalamus than that in children without the disorder. The main function of the thalamus is to relay motor and sensory signals to different areas of the brain. In adults with OCD, scans have found increased brain matter in the left orbitofrontal cortex, the area of the brain that is responsible for decision making and other cognitive processes.

NEUROTRANSMITTERS AND OCD

Researchers believe that OCD, along with several other anxiety disorders, can be triggered by chemical changes in the brain. Some research has found a link between neurotransmitters and OCD. Neurotransmitters are brain chemicals that send messages between the brain's nerve cells, or neurons. Scientists believe that

Sophisticated imaging technology has allowed scientists to study the structure and function of the brain in people with OCD, identifying several factors that may play a role in the disorder.

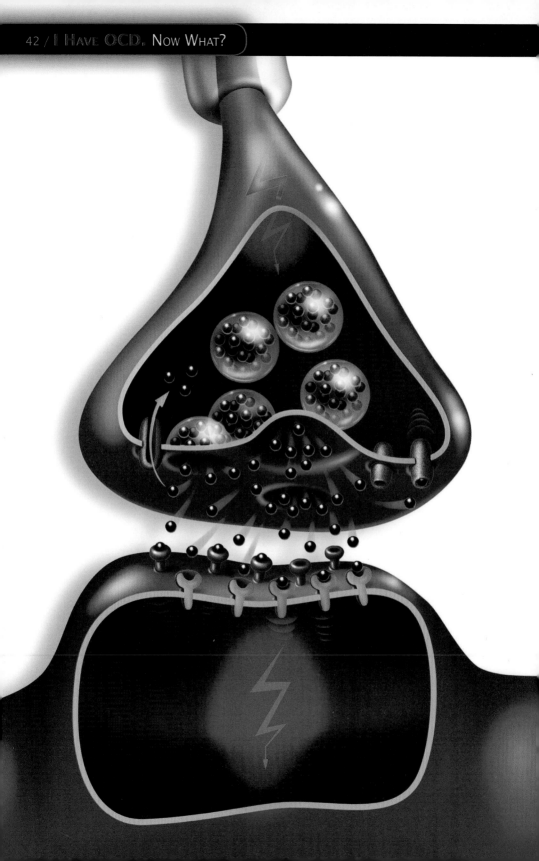

when the messages between neurons are mixed up and communication is disturbed, it may contribute to OCD and other mental disorders.

One neurotransmitter that has been linked to OCD is serotonin. Serotonin helps to regulate sleep, appetite, and mood. "Serotonin is one of the brain's chemical messengers that allow nerve cells to communicate, and we know that serotonin circuits are dysregulated in some of the individuals who have OCD," says Dr. Grice. Researchers believe that in patients with OCD, serotonin's timing is off and the brain's neurons do not fire signals the way that they should. As a result, communication between neurons does not take place effectively. When this happens to many neurons at the same time, symptoms of OCD appear.

Imbalances in other brain chemicals might also affect OCD. Dopamine is a neurotransmitter that works to regulate movement and emotions. When depleted, dopamine has been linked to Parkinson's disease and OCD. A hormone called vasopressin has also been studied for its possible links to OCD.

GENETIC FACTORS

Family history may also have a role in who develops OCD. Research in families shows that people have a

Brain chemicals called neurotransmitters transmit messages between the nerve cells in the brain. Scientists believe that disruptions in this message system may be a factor in OCD and other mental disorders.

A scientist studies the DNA sequence of a patient with OCD. Because OCD often runs in families, scientists believe that genes play a role in who develops OCD.

higher chance of developing the disorder if a parent or sibling also has OCD. According to the National Alliance on Mental Illness, about 25 percent of people diagnosed with OCD have a family member who has been diagnosed with the disorder.

Because of the family connection, researchers believe that genes may play a role in who develops OCD. In 2003, researchers in a National Institutes of Health–funded collaborative study discovered that OCD has a hereditary component. They discovered a mutated serotonin transporter gene called hSERT in unrelated families with OCD. A second OCD-related gene mutation was linked to severe symptoms. Other studies have also supported OCD's genetic link.

Studies of twins have found that identical twins were more than twice as likely to have OCD than fraternal twins.

In 2014, researchers at the Johns Hopkins University School of Medicine announced that they had identified a genetic marker that may be associated with the development of OCD. In a press release, the director of the school's Obsessive-Compulsive Disorder Program stated, "We might ultimately be able to identify new drugs that could help people with this often disabling disorder, one for which current medications work only 60 to 70 percent of the time." The researchers scanned the genomes of more than 1,400 people with OCD and more than 1,000 close relatives of people with the disorder. They identified a significant association for OCD patients near a gene called protein tyrosine phosphokinase. This gene has been linked to learning and memory in animals—traits that are also affected by OCD in humans. Furthermore, the gene has been associated with some cases of attention deficit hyperactivity disorder, which shares many symptoms with OCD. Researchers hope that this finding will lead to a better understanding of OCD and the development of more effective treatment.

Much work remains before researchers understand exactly how genes influence OCD. Scientists believe that OCD is not caused by a single gene. Instead, they think that several genes act together to contribute to OCD. In addition, researchers still believe that other factors, such as environment and brain chemistry, also play a role in determining who develops OCD.

For most people, OCD symptoms emerge gradually. A person begins to experience fears and anxiety. He or she tries to hide those fears and manage them with compulsive rituals such as counting, checking, or washing. Eventually, the fears become more intense, and the rituals consume more and more time until the person can no longer hide them.

However, for certain children, severe symptoms of OCD appear suddenly. These patients may also experience sudden mood swings, irritability, and anxiety. They might start wetting the bed or having trouble writing clearly. When this occurs, the child may be diagnosed with pediatric acute-onset neuropsychiatric syndrome (PANS).

Doctors do not know why PANS occurs. Some scientists believe that an infection may cause the child's body to develop antibodies that mistakenly target an area of the brain that controls behavior. Previously, scientists believed that acute-onset OCD could be triggered by a streptococcus infection, such as strep throat. However, in recent years, researchers believe that OCD symptoms could be triggered by other types of infections, including the flu, chicken pox, mycoplasma, and Lyme disease. The source of acute-onset symptoms may also be unknown.

While PANS is not contagious, the underlying infection that causes it may be. Scientists who are studying PANS hope to learn more about how infections, OCD, and symptoms are linked so that they can better treat the disorder.

ACUTE-ONSET OCD

ENVIRONMENTAL FACTORS

Although genetics and biology are important, some people develop OCD without any known family history of the disorder. Others with family members who have been diagnosed with OCD never develop it. Scientists believe that this variation occurs because environmental influences also play a role in influencing who develops OCD.

Some environmental factors that may affect the development of OCD include substance abuse, stress, injury, and learned habits. In some cases, OCD can be triggered by the stress of a specific and traumatic life event. Traumatic events such as the death of a loved one, the loss of a pet, or a divorce in the family can cause high levels

Stress caused by the death of a loved one or other traumatic experiences has been linked to OCD. Scientists are working to understand why stress can trigger OCD in some individuals but not others.

of stress. For those vulnerable to OCD, a combination of stressful events, genetics, and biology may trigger OCD.

Although stress can trigger OCD in certain people, it does not affect all people in the same way. Not everyone who develops OCD has experienced high levels of stress. Furthermore, the same stressful event may trigger OCD in one person but not in another.

Traumatic brain injury might also trigger the onset of OCD in some patients. Brain injury can be caused by car or other accidents, shootings, or falls. Damage to certain areas of the brain has been linked to the onset of OCD symptoms. OCD triggered by a brain injury usually appears soon after the event. Frequently, it is accompanied by symptoms of depression.

Family involvement can also influence the development of OCD. When a person with OCD becomes highly upset over his or her obsessions, family members might try to help by accommodating the person. They may constantly reassure the person that everything is all right. They may also enable the person to perform his or her rituals or help the affected family member avoid objects or situations that trigger his or her anxiety. Although the family members are trying to help, their efforts may actually cause the person's symptoms to become more severe. Accommodating a person with OCD can also damage family relationships and reinforce the affected individual's reliance on rituals or avoidance in the future.

MENTAL HEALTH HISTORY

Many people with OCD suffer from more than one mental illness. Having one disorder can increase a person's risk for developing another disorder. Common co-occurring disorders include depression, eating disorders, substance abuse, attention deficit hyperactivity disorder, and other anxiety and tic disorders. When a person has more than one mental illness, OCD is often harder to diagnose and treat.

According to the National Alliance for Mental Illness, researchers believe that OCD may be linked to such other mental disorders as anxiety disorders, Tourette's syndrome, and eating disorders, because each of these illnesses can be triggered by similar chemical changes in the brain. Research has shown that people with a family history of tic disorders such as Tourette's syndrome are at a higher risk of developing OCD. "OCD and tic disorders often co-occur, so anyone who has one of these disorders has an elevated risk to develop the other," says Dr. Grice in her interview with the *New York Daily News*. "Up to 30 percent of patients with OCD have a current or past history of tics, and up to 45 percent of patients with Tourette disorder also have OCD or OCD-related symptoms."

MULTIPLE FACTORS

Obsessive-compulsive disorder is an illness, but it is not always easy to identify and treat because it is not known

A person who has OCD may be at a greater risk for developing another mental illness, such as an eating disorder.

to be caused by a single factor. Instead, most scientists believe that a combination of biological, genetic, and environmental factors influence who develops OCD. Every person reacts differently to OCD's risk factors. The same factors may cause the development of OCD in some people while in others they do not. Although it is difficult to identify the precise cause of OCD in a given case, knowing the risk factors can help a person be more aware of the warning signs so that he or she seeks help when needed.

CHAPTER 4

GETTING TREATMENT: PSYCHOTHERAPY

Although there is no cure, obsessive-compulsive disorder is a treatable disease. According to the International OCD Foundation, most studies show that approximately 70 percent of people with OCD show an improvement in their symptoms with treatment. Although symptoms may become less severe with treatment, it is important to know that OCD is a chronic disease. Ongoing treatment is usually an important factor in making life with OCD easier to manage.

There are a variety of treatment options for people with OCD. Most people benefit from a combination of psychotherapy, medication, family support, and education. The earlier treatment begins, the more effective it can be in reducing symptoms. OCD treatment is not a quick fix. It can often takes anywhere from twelve to fourteen weeks before a patient notices an improvement in symptoms. Patience and persistence are important.

Sometimes a person with OCD can feel helpless. However, with treatment, most people with OCD see improvements in their symptoms.

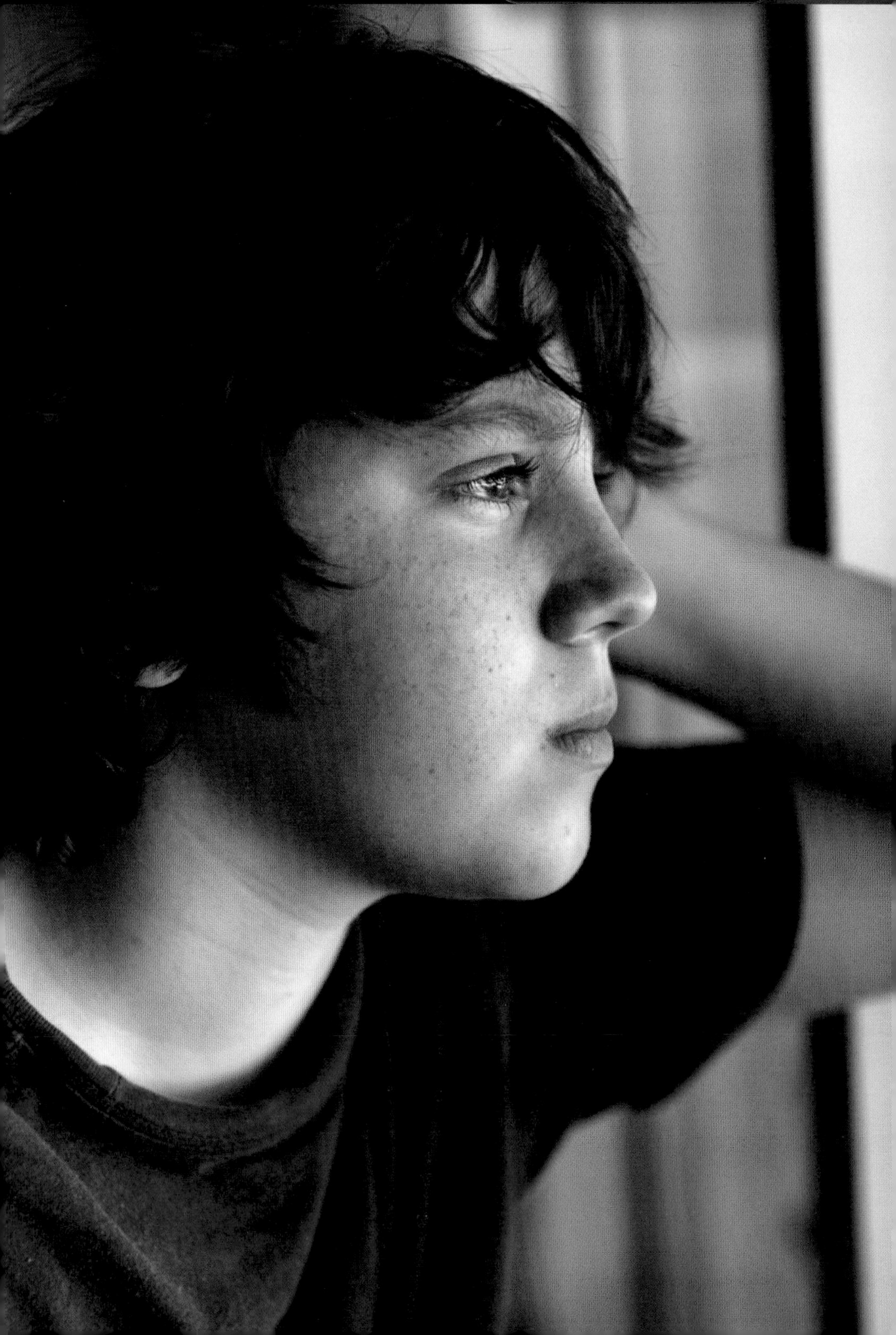

DIAGNOSING OCD

When a person experiences obsessions and compulsive behaviors, mental health experts recommend that the person seek professional help. Over time, untreated OCD can increasingly affect a person's ability to live a normal life. Obsessions interfere with daily life and decrease a person's ability to concentrate. Compulsions consume valuable time and drain both physical and mental energy. Some people are able to live with mild OCD without treatment. Over time, however, obsessions and compulsions are likely to take up more time

Seeing a doctor or other mental health professional can be the first step in learning to manage symptoms of OCD.

and energy, severely limiting a person's ability to study, to work, or to enjoy time with family and friends. People who do not seek treatment for OCD are at risk of social isolation, physical and emotional exhaustion, and failure at school or at work. They are also at risk of developing secondary disorders such as depression or substance abuse. In some extreme cases, untreated OCD can even lead to a person becoming completely incapacitated.

A trained doctor or mental health expert can diagnose patients with OCD. To diagnose obsessive-compulsive disorder, a mental health expert may do several exams. A physical exam may be done to rule out any other illnesses or physical conditions that might cause similar symptoms. Lab tests may be ordered to check a patient's blood count, screen for alcohol and drugs, and check thyroid function. In a psychological evaluation, a mental health professional will ask about a person's thoughts, feelings, and behaviors. Generally, a mental health professional is looking for three signs of OCD. Does the patient have obsessions? Does he or she perform compulsive behaviors? Do the obsessions and compulsions take up significant time and interfere with work, school, or socializing with friends and family? If OCD is diagnosed, patients will work with a mental health professional who has specialized training in the treatment of OCD in order to determine an appropriate treatment plan.

College student Clare M. says that she felt relieved when she was diagnosed with OCD because there was a name for the symptoms she had been experiencing and a treatment plan. Clare wrote about her experience for the Anxiety and Depression Association of America, saying, "When I discovered that I had something that was real and treatable, I experienced much relief. Finding the right therapist took some time and patience . . . But with the help of my excellent therapist . . . I was finally able to confront my fears. I learned how to fight OCD: Instead of hiding, I had to attack it head on." Through successful treatment, Clare was able to return to school and a normal life. It is a continuing battle, but one that a patient with the right tools can win. She says, "Even with treatment, I have to manage my OCD every day, but I've learned to cope and live with its presence."

PSYCHOTHERAPY

For many patients, psychotherapy—also called talk therapy—is a common treatment for OCD. Psychotherapy aims to relieve OCD symptoms and help patients manage their obsessions and compulsive behavior by helping them develop an understanding or insight into their problems. Psychotherapy can take place in individual, group, or family sessions. During a session, the patient talks to a mental health expert about his or her feelings and problems and learns strategies to deal with them.

One type of psychotherapy, called cognitive behavior therapy (CBT), has been proven particularly effective at treating OCD. According to the International OCD Foundation, patients who respond to CBT report a 60 to 80 percent reduction in their symptoms. CBT aims

Here a patient talks with a mental health counselor about her feelings and experiences with OCD and learns strategies to help her cope with symptoms.

to teach patients different ways of thinking, behaving, and reacting to common situations so that they feel less anxious or fearful and avoid obsessive thoughts. CBT is based on the idea that a person's thoughts influence his or her feelings and behaviors. Negative thoughts will lead to negative feelings and behaviors. Therefore, CBT focuses on changing a person's patterns of negative thinking. CBT has been proved to work for treating all forms of OCD.

EXPOSURE AND RESPONSE PREVENTION

One form of CBT, called exposure and response prevention (ERP), has proven exceptionally effective for treating patients with OCD. There are two components to this type of treatment: exposure therapy and response prevention. Exposure therapy forces a patient to face his or her fears repeatedly, until the fear decreases. Guided by a trained ERP therapist, a patient confronts the thoughts, images, objects, or situations that cause him or her anxiety. As the patient is repeatedly exposed to this fear, his or her behavioral and sensory responses decrease over time. This process is known as habituation. Habituation can be likened to when you jump into a cold swimming pool and the sensation of cold decreases after a few minutes. Your body adjusts to the shock of the cold temperature and becomes used to the cold. In the same way, exposure therapy uses habituation to treat OCD. When a patient is repeatedly exposed to something that causes him or her anxiety, habituation allows that person's anxiety and fear responses to gradually decrease.

During exposure therapy, a therapist may choose to increase the intensity of the exposure gradually. For example, a person being treated for contamination OCD may first touch a public doorknob. The patient experiences anxiety until it subsides. Next, the therapist might increase the difficulty or intensity of the exposure by taking the patient to a shopping mall. There, the patient touches more common surfaces that have been handled or touched by strangers. As habituation occurs and the patient's anxiety decreases, the next exposure exercise might be touching a doorknob in a public restroom. In this way, the patient repeatedly faces the objects and situations that cause anxiety. Through successful repeated exposure, the patient comes to learn that nothing dangerous or harmful will happen after touching a doorknob in public.

The second part of ERP is response prevention. People with OCD typically perform ritual behaviors because they reduce anxiety. Not performing a ritual when faced with the things that make him or her anxious can cause a patient's anxiety to soar. However, it is important that patients do not give in to their compulsive behaviors. Using the previous example of a patient with contamination OCD, after touching a public doorknob, that patient will likely feel the urge to wash his or her hands. It is important that he or she resist that urge. Response prevention eliminates the reward that a patient feels when he or she engages in a ritual behavior to reduce anxiety. When the behavior is no longer associated with a reward, it will eventually stop.

At first, ERP may sound scary to many patients with OCD. They are uncomfortable facing their fears head-on. For this reason, it is important to find a trained mental health professional who can carefully explain and guide ERP therapy. When patients understand how exposure and habituation work, they may be more willing to try ERP and deal with the initial anxiety produced by exposure therapy. ERP helps patients discover that their unreasonable fears will not come true. For example, a patient who repeatedly counts objects to prevent bad luck will learn that bad luck won't come his or her way if he or she fails to count objects. At first, the patient might be scared or anxious, but eventually that fear or anxiety will decrease as the patient becomes accustomed to those feelings and realizes that nothing bad will happen to him or her when the ritual is not performed.

Elizabeth McIngvale-Cegelski was diagnosed with OCD as a teen. In a May 2014 interview with ABC News, she shared, "I was taunted by intrusive thoughts that never seemed to end unless I ritualized—doing tasks over and over and over for hours at a time. Basic things like washing my hair had to be repeated until I thought it was done correctly. I would scrub my hands until the skin was raw. One round was never enough." McIngvale-Cegelski says that, eventually, she was able to manage her OCD through treatment and ERP therapy. This helped her regain control of her life. McIngvale-Cegelski turned her battle with OCD into a career, going on to graduate with a doctoral degree in social work after completing therapy. Regarding recovery, she said, "My battle wasn't easy and isn't over. I still battle my OCD on a daily basis but I learned the tools needed in order to successfully manage my illness and the life that I deserve to live. Treatment for OCD is available and it can get better."

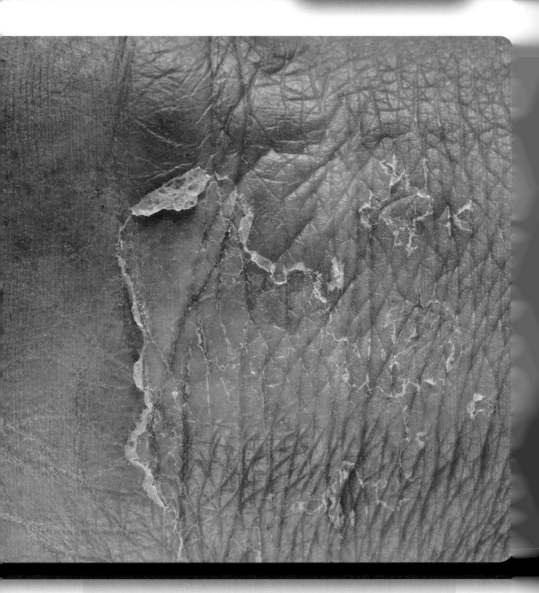

Some people with OCD wash their hands so often that their skin becomes raw. Through exposure and response prevention therapy, these individuals may overcome their need to wash and regain control of their lives.

OBSTACLES TO TREATMENT

Although treatment can be very effective at minimizing the impact of symptoms of OCD, many people face obstacles in determining which treatment works best for them. According to the International OCD Foundation, studies have found that it takes an average

DEEP BRAIN STIMULATION

An experimental procedure called deep brain stimulation may provide relief for some patients with severe OCD symptoms who haven't responded to other forms of treatment. Deep brain stimulation involves placing electrodes on targeted areas of the brain. The electrodes are connected by wires under the skin to a pulse generator, also located under the surface of the skin. The pulse generator acts as a pacemaker. It sends electrical signals to the brain. These electrical signals alter the electrical fields in those areas of the brain believed to be associated with the patient's symptoms of OCD. Using this procedure, doctors can precisely deliver electrical current to specific areas of the brains and soften the severity of OCD symptoms, thus helping patients respond better to conventional treatments.

While effective, this procedure is not without risks. There is a slight risk of internal bleeding in the brain, stroke, and infection from the surgery that implants the electrodes. Furthermore, a battery pack under the skin powers the pulse generator; this requires additional surgery to replace the batteries. Deep brain stimulation is generally reserved for extremely difficult or debilitating cases of obsessive-compulsive disorder.

of fourteen to seventeen years from the time that symptoms of OCD begin to appear before most patients first seek treatment. Many of those people who avoid seeking treatment do so because they are embarrassed. They choose to hide their symptoms—causing them not to seek help for many years. In addition, for many years there was little public awareness of OCD. Many people weren't aware that their symptoms were indicative of a mental disorder that could be treated.

Even when patients do seek treatment, OCD can be difficult to diagnose. Its symptoms can be similar to such varied mental disorders as obsessive-compulsive personality disorder, anxiety, depression, or schizophrenia. Many people with OCD have co-occurring disorders (multiple disorders whose symptoms overlap), further complicating diagnosis. As a result, many patients with symptoms of OCD will spend several years in treatment before receiving a correct diagnosis and starting an appropriate treatment plan.

10 GREAT QUESTIONS TO ASK A THERAPIST

1. What techniques and treatments do you recommend to treat OCD?

2. What is your training and background in treating OCD?

3. How much of your practice currently involves working with patients with OCD?

4. How many of your patients are currently being treated for anxiety disorders other than OCD?

5. With how many of your patients have you used cognitive behavioral therapy (CBT) to treat OCD?

6. What success rate have you noticed in your patients with OCD who have undergone CBT?

7. Do you use exposure and response prevention (ERP) to treat OCD?

8. What role do you think medication has in the treatment of OCD?

9. How long should I expect it to take before I notice an improvement in my symptoms after starting treatment?

10. Are you able to meet outside your office for CBT and/or ERP?

For some patients, doctors prescribe medication to treat OCD. Because many scientists believe that OCD may be linked to an imbalance in brain chemicals, medication works to level out imbalanced chemical levels in the brain. Correcting this imbalance can help reduce obsessive thoughts and compulsive behaviors. Medication is not necessary for all OCD patients, but it might be helpful for some. According to the International OCD Foundation, patients who respond to medication usually show between a 40 and 60 percent reduction in OCD symptoms. In many cases, a treatment plan that combines medication and psychotherapy helps many patients manage their OCD symptoms.

Types of Medications

Anti-anxiety medications and antidepressants are the most commonly prescribed medications for OCD. Antianxiety medications are powerful drugs that frequently begin working right away to relieve OCD symptoms and anxiety. However, these powerful medications are generally not recommended for use over long periods of time.

A particular group of antidepressants called selective serotonin reuptake inhibitors (SSRIs)

For many people, doctor-prescribed anti-depressants or antianxiety medications form part of a treatment plan that helps them successfully manage their OCD symptoms.

is also commonly prescribed to help patients manage OCD symptoms. SSRIs are typically used to treat depressive disorders, but they have been shown to help relieve symptoms of OCD. These medications work by adjusting chemicals in the brain such as serotonin. Serotonin is used by the brain as a messenger and has been linked to OCD.

As with many medications, antidepressants take time to start working. For most people, the medications accumulate in their systems over a period of several weeks—even ten to twelve weeks for some patients—before they start working. It can also take time to find the right medication or dosage that works for each

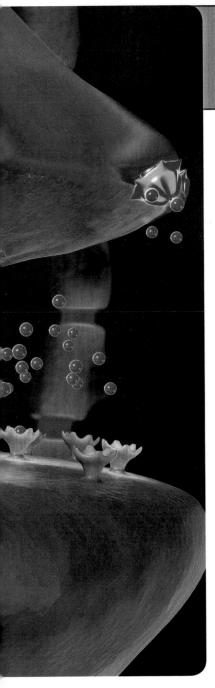

Antidepressant medications work by adjusting chemicals that may be out of balance in the brain, allowing the brain to function more effectively.

person's brain chemistry and symptoms. If the first medication prescribed doesn't work, the doctor may adjust the dosage or prescribe a different antidepressant.

In some cases, the mental health professional may prescribe a second medication to improve results. For some patients, augmenting, or supplementing, treatment with a second medication can help address specific OCD symptoms that the first medication may not be addressing. For example, some patients taking an SSRI may also be prescribed an antianxiety medication. Augmentation can be used when a patient has a coexisting depression, tic disorder, or other mental disorder. Augmentation may also be used when a patient shows persistent anxiety, even while taking an antidepressant.

WHO TREATS OCD?

Many mental health professionals can diagnose and treat obsessive-compulsive disorder. Primary care doctors are often part of a patient's initial diagnosis. They may refer a patient to a mental health specialist. There are several types of mental health specialists who can treat obsessive-compulsive disorder. Psychiatrists are medical doctors who diagnose and treat OCD. They can write prescriptions and provide psychotherapy. Psychologists have doctoral degrees in psychology. They can diagnose, treat, and monitor patients with OCD, but they cannot prescribe medications. Nurse practitioners are nurses with advanced training. They can diagnose OCD, prescribe medication, and provide therapy. Other professionals who may be involved in treating patients with OCD include licensed mental health counselors and social workers. Regardless of the type of health professional, it is important that they have experience diagnosing and treating patients with obsessive-compulsive disorder. Always ask a trusted primary care doctor for a referral. Don't be afraid to ask about a mental health professional's background in treating OCD before deciding upon an appropriate treatment program.

SIDE EFFECTS

Medication such as antidepressants and antianxiety drugs do have side effects. Most patients experience at least one or more side effects. For many people, side effects are not a great problem, especially if they

As with most medications, there are side effects associated with antidepressants and other medications used to treat OCD. Medications affect everyone differently, and patients should discuss any side effects with their doctors.

begin the medication at a low dosage and then slowly increase it over time. Many side effects are mild, while others can be more disruptive. Side effects often include nausea, fatigue, weight gain or loss, insomnia, dizziness, dry mouth, or headache. Some medications may also

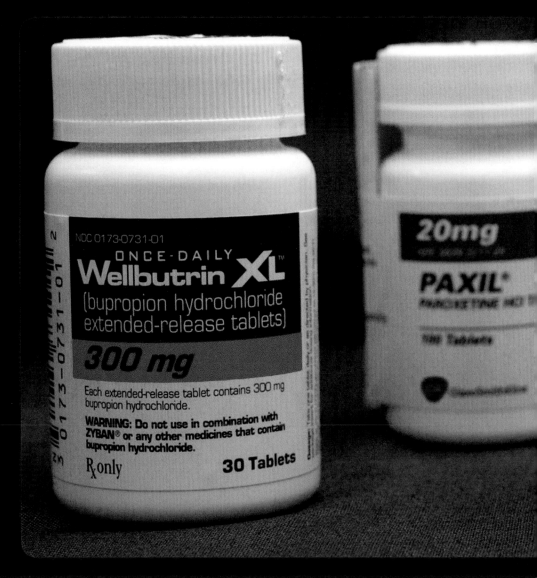

Although the medications used to treat OCD are generally safe, there can be serious side effects in certain individuals. Patients should carefully read all labels and warnings and communicate with their doctors regarding any bothersome side effects.

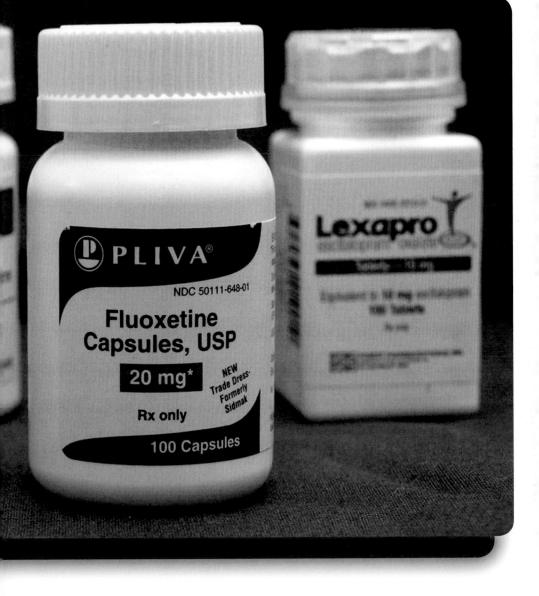

cause urinary retention (difficulty urinating), decreased sex drive, tremors, and nervousness. Some side effects are temporary, while others are more lasting. If side effects are making a patient uncomfortable, he or she should discuss these concerns with a doctor. The patient and doctor can work together to assess the benefits of medication against the side effects. The doctor may lower the dosage or switch the patient to a different medication.

In order for medication to work, patients must take it regularly and as directed. Nearly 50 percent of OCD patients stop taking their medication without consulting their doctors because of the side effects or other undesirable factors, which can lead to the return or worsening of symptoms. Suddenly stopping medication can have serious consequences. Stopping medication can trigger withdrawal symptoms or a bout of anxiety or depression. It is important to talk to a doctor before stopping medication or making changes to prescribed dosages. A doctor should be able to help a patient manage medication to reduce side effects by either adjusting the dosage or using a different type of medication that is better tolerated by a patient's body.

Although antidepressants can be safe and effective for some people, they may be risky for others. In recent years, the United States Food and Drug Administration (FDA) has placed a "black box warning" on many of the antidepressant medications used to treat OCD and other mental disorders. A black box warning is the most serious warning that a prescription drug can carry.

The FDA warns that there may be an increased risk of suicidal thoughts and behaviors in the first weeks of treatment with these medications. Patients who take antidepressants should be monitored closely, particularly at the start of treatment. A person who is thinking about taking medication to manage OCD symptoms should have an in-depth discussion with his or her mental health professional about the risks and benefits of starting any medication.

WHAT TO EXPECT FROM MEDICATION

Most OCD medications are generally started at a low dosage and then gradually increased depending on the patient's response. A patient who begins treatment with medication should expect to stay on the drugs for at least a year. Most researchers say that unless the medication is taken for one to two years after symptoms are under control, the patient's risk of relapse is high. Not everyone is the same, however, and some will be treated for longer periods while others will stop medication after a shorter period of time. There is no way to predict which medication or combination of medications will be the most effective for a patient. That is why it is important for patients and their doctors to work together to determine the best medication plan.

For treatment to be successful, it is imperative to follow the treatment plan developed by a mental health professional. Some patients stop taking medication or skip psychotherapy sessions because they are feeling better or do not like the side effects. According to the International OCD Foundation, at least 25 percent of OCD patients refuse to participate in cognitive behavioral therapy and nearly 50 percent of patients stop taking their medication without first discussing it with their health care professional. For many of these people, OCD symptoms will return. Experts caution that medicines have to be taken on a regular basis and patients must participate in CBT or ERP for treatment to be successful.

OCD is a chronic disease. Symptoms may be mild at times and more severe at others. Although there is no cure for OCD, there are effective treatments that can make it easier to manage. With medication and psychotherapy, people with OCD can manage symptoms and live productive lives.

CHAPTER 6

Although there is no cure for OCD, it can be treated effectively. In order to live successfully with OCD, you will need to learn how to manage it. Your mental health professional can help you discover the best strategies that work for you to cope with your symptoms. Over time, you will learn what strategies work best to manage your OCD so that you can live a productive and normal life.

HEALTHY LIFESTYLE

Lifestyle can have a big impact on how you feel. Certain lifestyle choices can help you feel better and more easily manage your symptoms. When you do not take care of yourself, you are more susceptible to fatigue, sleep problems, tension, stress, and difficulties with concentration. These problems can make you more vulnerable to anxiety and worsen your OCD-related symptoms. On the contrary, having a healthy lifestyle can make it easier for you to manage anxiety and symptoms of OCD. Making sure that you eat well, exercise, and get enough sleep are all good ways to keep your body in balance. Starting the day with breakfast and

Exercise such as jogging and other physical activities can release chemicals called endorphins in the brain that make you feel good and reduce stress and anxiety.

eating regular, healthy meals throughout the day can keep your blood sugar levels stable, which can reduce anxiety. Eating complex carbohydrates such as whole grains, fruits, and vegetables also stabilizes blood sugar and increases levels of the neurotransmitter serotonin, which can improve mood and calmness.

Boost Your Endorphins

Exercise, in particular, is a powerful tool to help reduce stress and anxiety. Exercise releases chemicals called endorphins into the brain—a natural way to feel good. In many cases, exercise is a social activity. Getting out to an exercise class or playing basketball with friends is a great way to build social support networks. For patients with OCD, exercise can also be a distraction, taking their minds off obsessions and compulsions. For maximum benefit, experts recommend at least thirty minutes of aerobic exercise on most days.

In one study performed at Brown University's Alpert Medical School, researchers studied the impact of aerobic exercise on symptoms of OCD. In the study, patients with OCD continued their usual treatment program of medication and therapy but also participated in a twelve-week moderate-intensity exercise program. At the end of the twelve-week aerobic exercise program, researchers found that the frequency and severity of the patients' OCD symptoms had decreased. Furthermore, this improvement in symptoms lasted over a follow-up period of six months. Patients who participated in the study also reported an improvement in their overall sense of well-being.

Catch Some Zs

Sleeping too little or too much can make it harder to manage the symptoms of OCD. Experts recommend that most people try to get between seven and eight hours of sleep each night. When a person is well rested, it is easier to keep emotions in balance, which affects how an individual copes with anxiety. Going to bed and waking up at the same time every day can help establish healthy sleep habits. If you have problems sleeping, you may want to talk to your doctor about possible solutions or treatment for insomnia.

Getting regular sleep can help keep OCD symptoms at bay. Doctors recommend getting between seven and eight hours of sleep each night. A regular sleep schedule can also contribute to better management of OCD symptoms.

Following a regular daily routine can make it easier to manage OCD symptoms. Setting specific times for meals, work or school, chores, quiet time, and bedtime will help create a daily routine. Following a routine makes the day's events more predictable, which in turn reduces stress. A consistent routine can also help you get things done and remind you to make taking time for yourself a priority in your day.

MANAGING STRESS

Managing stress is another way to reduce vulnerability to anxiety. Stressful events can trigger OCD symptoms and make them worse. Experts say that excess stress makes it more difficult for you to find solutions, make productive choices, and have the energy to manage symptoms.

There are several techniques that you can use to reduce stress in your life. Some people use art and writing as a way to release stress. Others focus on simplifying and cutting back on unnecessary activities, staying positive, and learning to recognize the warning signs of stress. Others practice meditation, yoga, or deep-breathing techniques that help calm the mind and body. Practicing some form of relaxation technique for at least thirty minutes a day can help you manage your symptoms more easily.

Hobbies such as writing, painting, and other crafts can reduce stress and consequently lessen the severity of OCD symptoms. This is because when stress levels are low, a person is less vulnerable to anxiety and better able to control obsessions.

What if you suspect a friend or family member has obsessive-compulsive disorder? What should you do? Experts say that the best thing you can do to help someone who you suspect has OCD is to encourage him or her to seek proper treatment. The person may be too embarrassed to ask for help. Or that person might be trying to hide his or her symptoms and rituals. If you notice changes in behavior that are disrupting the person's everyday activities, he or she should be evaluated by a professional. Be gentle—not confrontational—and show your care for the person as well as your knowledge about the disorder.

Learning more about OCD can be the biggest help. Educating yourself with real facts about the disorder and its symptoms can help you deal with the person more effectively and understand his or her thoughts and behaviors. Knowledge about the treatment of OCD can also help you find strategies to help your friend or family member overcome his or her obsessions and compulsive behavior.

Many people think they are helping the most by allowing a friend or family member to avoid anxiety-producing situations or helping him or her perform compulsive rituals. While accommodating him or her may reduce a person's anxiety in the short term, over time it is likely to make the symptoms of OCD worse.

FIND A SUPPORT SYSTEM

Another key to managing OCD successfully is to get support. Sometimes, the obsessions and compulsions of OCD can make you feel alone. A good support system can help you cope with symptoms as they occur. Support may come from family, friends, a therapist, or a support

Sometimes just having a friend to talk to can help reduce anxiety and help a person cope with symptoms as they occur.

group of other people who have also experienced OCD. Many people find that joining a support group and meeting others with similar experiences helps them better manage their symptoms. Some support groups meet in person, while others are over the phone or online. Support groups allow you to share your experiences and learn from others who are dealing with the same problems. Your therapist or other mental health professional can recommend support groups in your area that will connect you with others who understand the challenges of OCD firsthand.

In addition to support groups, there are several organizations that are dedicated to helping people with OCD. These groups work to educate people about OCD, how it is diagnosed, and how it is treated. Some also support research into learning more about the causes of OCD and new approaches to treatment.

LEARNING ABOUT OCD

No matter what form of OCD you may have, it is important to learn as much as you can about the disorder. With knowledge, you can make informed decisions about your treatment and how to manage your symptoms. There are many books and articles that provide a wealth

The more a person learns about OCD, the better equipped he or she will be to handle symptoms and challenges as they arise.

of information about the disorder. You can ask your mental health professionals for recommendations of books, articles, and websites where you can learn more about managing your specific type of OCD.

Organizations devoted to OCD and other mental health issues are another excellent source of information. The International OCD Foundation is a nonprofit organization that is dedicated to helping people with OCD and related disorders live full and productive lives. The organization was founded in 1986 by a group of patients diagnosed with OCD. Today, it is an international organization with chapters in twenty-five U.S. states and around the world. The foundation works to help people with OCD get access to treatment. It also promotes awareness about OCD and educates patients and the public about the disorder. Information on this and similar organizations can be found at the back of this resource.

LIVING WITH OCD

It is completely possible to manage your OCD and live a full life. For more than ten years, Becky Wolsk suffered from symptoms of OCD. Afraid of harming someone, she compulsively checked coffeemakers to ensure they were turned off and wouldn't start an electrical fire. She painstakingly checked anything that she wrote to make sure that she hadn't written anything embarrassing or unkind. She also worried about food contamination to the extent that she became unable to enjoy cooking anymore.

Unable to manage her symptoms on her own, Wolsk began medication in February 2006. She immediately felt relief. She participated in behavioral therapy and read everything she could find about her disorder. Wolsk also concentrated on establishing a healthy lifestyle to reduce stress and improve her symptoms. She found that she could reduce her stress levels by studying several religious and spiritual traditions, including Judaism, Christianity, Buddhism, and Taoism. She also practices yoga and eats a healthy diet. Wolsk believes that the most important thing is to be kind to yourself as you learn to live with OCD. "Try to treat yourself gently, especially when you think you did a bad thing by giving in to compulsions," she said in an article for the Anxiety and Depression Association of America. "Lapses are part of recovery, not the loss of it. The tyrant [or, demanding voice] in your head will second-guess you no matter what you do. That voice of dread is terrified, terrifying, loud, and repetitively destructive. Demote it by making it your pesky backseat driver. You can steer without it. If you feel like you keep falling, just keep getting up. Anxiety will always accompany us, but it doesn't have to be excessive. You'll learn to distrust the scolding voice in your head, instead of doubting yourself," she advises. By quieting the demanding voice in her own thoughts, Wolsk became able to manage the symptoms of her OCD and control her own life.

With a strong support system and with proper treatment, most people with OCD learn to manage their symptoms and live active, healthy lives.

Finding Hope

In any form, OCD is a serious mental disorder. It is, however, treatable. Many patients with OCD successfully manage their symptoms with a combination of psychotherapy, lifestyle changes, and, for some, medication. They build a strong support system that can help during difficult times, and they learn about their disorder. Because OCD affects each person in a unique way, it may take time for a patient to find the right combination of treatment options that works for him or her. Relief may not happen overnight, but it can happen. With treatment, everyone with OCD can have hope.

GLOSSARY

adherence The act of remaining firmly attached or bound to a practice or observance.

antidepressants Drugs that are used to treat major depressive disorder and other mental illnesses including obsessive-compulsive disorder.

anxiety A feeling of fear, unease, and worry that is experienced by people with obsessive-compulsive disorder.

augmentation The addition of another medication to a patient's treatment plan in order to improve treatment results.

compelled Forced to do something that one does not want to do.

compulsion An irresistible urge to behave in a certain way, even if one does not want to do so.

contamination The act of making something unclean or impure by contact with something unclean or dirty.

disorder An abnormal condition that affects the body or organs of an individual.

gene The basic physical unit of heredity inside every cell.

habituation A form of learning in which an individual decreases a response to a certain stimulus after repeated exposure.

heredity The process of passing traits from parents to offspring.

hoarding A behavior in which people accumulate food or other items in unnecessarily large quantities.

intrusive Describes something that causes disruption or annoyance because it is unwanted or uninvited.

neurotransmitter Brain chemical that carries information from one neuron to another.

obsession The domination of an individual's mind by a particular thought, image, or desire.

psychotherapy The practice of spending time with a trained mental health therapist to talk about an individual's feelings and problems.

quell To reduce, calm, or quiet something, such as a fear.

ritual A sequence of actions or words that are performed in a specific order.

serotonin One of the brain's chemicals that has a role in regulating mood.

side effects Secondary, usually undesirable effects of a drug or medical treatment.

symmetrical Having sides that are the same and balanced.

therapist A person trained in psychology who is able to help patients manage and overcome mental disorders.

FOR MORE INFORMATION

American Academy of Child and Adolescent Psychiatry
    (AACAP)
3615 Wisconsin Avenue NW
Washington, DC 20016
(202) 966-7300
Website: http://www.aacap.org
The AACAP is a national professional medical
    association dedicated to treating and improving the
    quality of life for children, adolescents, and families
    affected by mental, behavioral, or developmental
    disorders.

American Institute of Stress (AIS)
6387B Camp Bowie Boulevard #334
Fort Worth, TX 76116
(682) 239-6823
Website: http://www.stress.org
The AIS is a nonprofit organization that imparts infor-
    mation on stress reduction, the effects of stress, and
    various other stress-related topics.

American Psychiatric Association
1000 Wilson Boulevard, Suite 1825
Arlington, VA 22209
(888) 357-7924
Website: http://www.psych.org

The American Psychiatric Association has more than 38,000 member physicians working together to ensure humane care and effective treatment for all persons with mental disorders.

American Psychological Association
750 First Street NE
Washington, DC 20002
(800) 374-2721
Website: http://www.apa.org
The American Psychological Association represents more than 148,000 professional American psychologists who study and treat human behavior.

Association for Behavioral and Cognitive Therapies (ABCT)
305 Seventh Avenue, 16th Floor
New York, NY 10001
(212) 647-1890
Website: http://www.abct.org
This association represents therapists who provide cognitive behavioral therapy for patients suffering from mental illness, including OCD.

Canadian Mental Health Association (CMHA)
1110-151 Slater Street
Ottawa, ON K1P 5H3
Canada
(613) 745-7750

Website: http://www.cmha.ca

As a nationwide, voluntary organization, the CMHA promotes the mental health of all and supports the recovery of people experiencing mental illness. It promotes advocacy, education, research, and service.

Canadian OCD Network (COCDN)
938 West 28th Avenue, A3-118
Vancouver, BC V5Z 4H4
Canada
Website: http://canadianocdnetwork.com

The COCDN is dedicated to increasing awareness and support for those who suffer from obsessive-compulsive disorder. The network aims to achieve increased public recognition, earlier diagnosis, and easier access to OCD treatment.

Health Canada
Address Locator 0900C2
Ottawa, ON
K1A 0K9
Canada
(866) 225-0709
Website: http://www.hc-sc.gc.ca

Health Canada is the federal department responsible for helping the people of Canada maintain and improve their physical and mental health.

International OCD Foundation
112 Water Street, Suite 501
Boston, MA 02109
(617) 973-5801
Website: http://www.iocdf.org
The International OCD Foundation is a not-for-profit
    organization that educates health care professionals
    and the public about OCD, supports research into
    the causes of OCD and its effective treatment, and
    promotes access to resources for people with OCD.

Mental Health America (MHA)
2000 North Beauregard Street, 6th Floor
Alexandria, VA 22311
(800) 969-6642
Website: http://www.mentalhealthamerica.net
MHA is an advocacy group for people with mental
    illnesses and their families. It provides such resources
    as fact sheets and listings of local support groups.

National Alliance on Mental Illness (NAMI)
3803 North Fairfax Drive, Suite 100
Arlington, VA 22203
(703) 524-7600
Website: http://www.nami.org
NAMI advocates for people with mental illnesses at local
    chapters in every state. It offers educational programs
    and services for individuals and family members.

National Institute of Mental Health (NIMH)
6001 Executive Boulevard, Room 8184, MSC 9663
Bethesda, MD 20892
(866) 615-6464
Website: http://www.nimh.nih.gov
NIMH is the federal government's chief funding agency
for mental health research in the United States. It
provides fact sheets and information about mental
illnesses, including OCD.

WEBSITES

Because of the changing nature of Internet links, Rosen
Publishing has developed an online list of websites
related to the subject of this book. This site is updated
regularly. Please use this link to access the list:

http://www.rosenlinks.com/411/OCD

FOR FURTHER READING

Baer, Lee. *Getting Control: Overcoming Your Obsessions and Compulsions.* New York, NY: Plume, 2012.

Bakewell, Lisa, ed. *Mental Health Information for Teens: Health Tips About Mental Wellness and Mental Illness, Including Facts About Recognizing and Treating Mood, Anxiety, Personality, Psychotic, Behavioral, Impulse Control, and Addiction Disorders.* Detroit, MI: Omnigraphics, 2014.

Berlatsky, Noah. *Mental Illness.* Detroit, MI: Greenhaven Press, 2013.

Bloom, Sheri, and Suzanne Mouton-Odum. *Out of the Rabbit Hole: A Road Map to Freedom from OCD.* Houston, TX: Wonderland, 2013.

Carlson, Dale, and Michael Bower. *Out of Order: Young Adult Manual of Mental Illness and Recovery: Mental Illnesses, Personality Disorders, Learning Problems, Intellectual Disabilities & Treatment and Recovery.* Branford, CT: Bick, 2013.

Carmin, Cheryl Nina, and Anne Coulter. *Obsessive-Compulsive Disorder Demystified: An Essential Guide for Understanding and Living with OCD.* Cambridge, MA: Da Capo Press, 2009.

Challacombe, Fiona, Victoria Bream Oldfield, and Paul M. Salkovskis. *Break Free from OCD.* London, UK: Vermilion, 2011.

Cozic, Charles P. *Teenage Mental Illness*. San Diego, CA: ReferencePoint, 2011.

Davidson, Joan, Ph.D. *Daring to Challenge OCD: Overcome Your Fear of Treatment & Take Control of Your Life Using Exposure & Response Prevention*. Oakland, CA: New Harbinger Publications, 2014.

Grayson, Jonathan. *Freedom from Obsessive-Compulsive Disorder: A Personalized Recovery Program for Living with Uncertainty*. New York, NY: Penguin Books, 2014.

Hyman, Bruce M., and Cherry Pedrick. *Obsessive-Compulsive Disorder*. Minneapolis, MN: Twenty-First Century, 2011.

Hyman, Bruce M., and Cherry Pedrick. *The OCD Workbook: Your Guide to Breaking Free from Obsessive-Compulsive Disorder*. Oakland, CA: New Harbinger Publications, 2010.

Iorizzo, Carrie. *Anxiety and Phobias*. New York, NY: Crabtree Publishing, 2014.

Leitch, Hayley, and Veronica Clark. *Coming Clean: Living with OCD*. London, UK: John Blake Publishing, 2014.

Parks, Peggy J. *Obsessive-Compulsive Disorder*. San Diego, CA: ReferencePoint, 2011.

Poskitt, Helen. *The Essential Guide to OCD: Help for Families and Friends*. Oxford, UK: Lion Hudson, 2012.

Schab, Lisa M. *The Anxiety Workbook for Teens: Activities to Help You Deal with Anxiety & Worry*. Oakland, CA: New Harbinger Publications, 2008.

Sisemore, Timothy A. *Free from OCD: A Workbook for Teens with Obsessive-Compulsive Disorder*. Oakland, CA: New Harbinger Publications, 2010.

Tompkins, Michael A., and Katherine A. Martinez. *My Anxious Mind: A Teen's Guide to Managing Anxiety and Panic*. Washington, DC: Magination Press, 2009.

Watkins, Heidi. *Obsessive-Compulsive Disorder*. Farmington Hills, MI: Greenhaven Press, 2010.

Willard, Christopher. *Mindfulness Workbook for Teen Anxiety: Manage Your Anxiety at Home, School, Social Situations and Daily Life*. Oakland, CA: New Harbinger Publications, 2014.

BIBLIOGRAPHY

Adam, David. "The Nightmare of Living with OCD." *Guardian*, April 4, 2014. Retrieved November 11, 2014 (http://www.theguardian.com/lifeandstyle/2014/apr/04/living-with-ocd-david-adam).

American Psychiatric Association. "Obsessive Compulsive Disorder." Retrieved November 11, 2014 (http://www.psychiatry.org/mental-health/obsessive-compulsive-disorder).

American Psychological Association. Retrieved November 11, 2014 (http://www.apa.org).

Anxiety and Depression Association of America. "Obsessive-Compulsive Disorder." Retrieved November 11, 2014 (http://www.adaa.org/understanding-anxiety/obsessive-compulsive-disorder-ocd).

Beyond OCD. Retrieved November 11, 2014 (http://www.beyondocd.org).

Carmin, Cheryl, Ph.D. *Obsessive-Compulsive Disorder Demystified: An Essential Guide for Understanding and Living with OCD*. Cambridge, MA: Da Capo Press, 2009.

Charles, Katie. "Obsessive-Compulsive Disorder Is a Leading Cause of Disability Worldwide, with Causes Not Fully Understood." *New York Daily News*, July 21, 2013. Retrieved November 11, 2014 (http://www.nydailynews.com/life-style/health/types-treatment-fight-ocd-article-1.1399477).

The Dana Foundation. Retrieved November 11, 2014
(http://www.dana.org/Publications/GuideDetails
.aspx?id=50035).

Graves, Ginny. "Is My OCD Habit a Health Problem?"
Health.com, March 9, 2009. Retrieved November
11, 2014 (http://www.health.com/health/
article/0,,20411571,00.html).

International OCD Foundation. Retrieved November 11,
2014 (http://www.iocdf.org).

Johns Hopkins Medicine. "Researchers Identify
Genetic Marker Linked to OCD." May 13,
2014. Retrieved November 11, 2014 (http://
www.hopkinsmedicine.org/news/media/releases/
researchers_identify_genetic_marker_linked_to_ocd).

M., Clare. "My Success Over OCD." Anxiety and
Depression Association of America. Retrieved
November 11, 2014 (http://www.adaa.org/living
-with-anxiety/personal-stories/my-success-over-ocd).

McIngvale-Cegelski, Elizabeth. "Living with OCD: The
Lifelong Battle for Control over the Disorder." ABC
News, May 22, 2014. Retrieved November 11,
2014 (http://abcnews.go.com/Health/living-ocd
-lifelong-battle-control-disorder/story?id=23811937
&singlePage=true).

Mental Health America. "Obsessive-Compulsive Disorder
(OCD)." Retrieved November 11, 2014 (http://www
.mentalhealthamerica.net/conditions/ocd).

National Alliance on Mental Health. Retrieved November
11, 2014 (http://www.nami.org).

National Institute of Mental Health. "What Is Obsessive-
Compulsive Disorder (OCD)?" Retrieved November
11, 2014 (http://www.nimh.nih.gov/health/topics/
obsessive-compulsive-disorder-ocd/index.shtml).

Shapiro, Benjamin. "OCD Is No Longer in Charge:
One Kid's Story." *Psychology Today*, May 6, 2014.
Retrieved November 11, 2014 (http://www
.psychologytoday.com/blog/the-guest-room/201405
/ocd-is-no-longer-in-charge-one-kid-s-story).

Teen Mental Health. Retrieved November 11, 2014
(http://www.teenmentalhealth.org).

Wolsk, Becky. "Working Toward Compassion and
Moderation." Anxiety and Depression Association of
America. Retrieved November 11, 2014 (http://www
.adaa.org/living-with-anxiety/personal-stories/
working-toward-compassion-and-moderation).

INDEX

A

acute-onset OCD, 47
antianxiety medications, 69, 73, 74
  side effects of, 74, 76, 78
antidepressants, 69, 71, 73, 74, 78, 79
  side effects of, 74, 76, 78
anxiety, 4, 6, 8, 10, 12, 14–15, 26, 28, 29, 35, 36, 39, 47, 50, 59, 61, 62–64, 67, 69, 73, 78, 81, 83, 85, 87, 88, 93
anxiety disorders, 41, 51, 68
attention deficit hyperactivity disorder, 46, 51

B

biological basis, of OCD, 38–39, 41, 50, 53
brain, role of in OCD, 8, 38–39, 41, 43, 46, 47, 51, 66, 69, 71, 73, 83
  injuries, 50

C

cognitive behavioral therapy (CBT), 59, 61–62, 68, 80
compulsions, 6, 8, 12
  checking, 13, 14, 24, 26, 28–29, 31, 47, 92

concentration, difficulties with, 56, 81

D

depression, 50, 51, 58, 67, 73, 78
diagnosing OCD, 4, 6, 14, 19, 21, 22, 44, 47, 48, 51, 56, 58–59, 64, 67, 74, 90, 92
distress, 8, 14, 15, 33–34
dopamine, 43

E

eating disorders, 51
education, importance in OCD treatment, 54, 88
endorphins, 83
environmental factors, in the development of OCD, 48, 50, 53
exercise, 83, 85
exposure and response prevention (ERP), 61–64, 68, 80

F

family involvement, role in the development of OCD, 50
family support, importance for OCD treatment, 54
fatigue, 76, 81

ABOUT THE AUTHOR

Carla Mooney is a graduate of the University of Pennsylvania. She is the author of many books for young adults and children. She enjoys learning about the brain and mental health.

PHOTO CREDITS